WHO YOU SAY I AM
YOU ARE LIFE
THE PASSION
GOD SO LOVED
BE STILL
REMEMBRANCE
VALENTINE
TOUCH OF HEAVEN
LETTERED LOVE
THE LORD'S PRAYER
NEW WINE
SO WILL I
(100 BILLION X)

Hillsong Worship - Our Hillsong Worship album is the combined effort of our Hillsong Church worship teams to express both our personal devotion and a congregational offering of worship. Ever-committed to resourcing individuals, worship teams and churches alike, the Hillsong Worship team seeks to bring songs that are as diverse as the greater Church herself is. Our prayer each year is that our Hillsong Worship album would offer songs for all generations and demographics that are declarations of faith and adoration.

UNITED & Y&F Teams - UNITED is committed to writing songs that speak truth, create a unique sound, connect with churches, individuals and ultimately connect people everywhere with God. Young & Free (Y&F) is the creative worship expression of Hillsong Church's current youth movement. Both the UNITED and Y&F teams serve in church as a part of the wider Hillsong Worship and Creative team when they are home. When on tour, they are accompanied by the whole Hillsong team's support and prayers that their ministry would arrest hearts and point people to Jesus, impacting individuals, local youth groups and local churches.

We are a church committed to inspiring and empowering the authentic worship of Jesus and resourcing the body of Christ. There are numerous resources we as Hillsong make available including inspiring teaching and books by Brian & Bobbie Houston, curriculum content that can impact your children's, outreach and discipleship ministries, and of course music. For more information visit hillsongmusic.com

We are a church that believes in championing the cause of the local church. Hillsong Conference is about you, your church and seeing God's Kingdom advance across the earth. This is your chance to lean in, receive and take home practical teachings you can outwork in your own church home, family and community. It's about being refreshed and inspired and finding great strength and unity amongst the diversity of the local church worldwide. For more information visit hillsongconference.com

We are a church that believes in placing value upon womanhood. Colour Conference, at the very core is a strong humanitarian message. Our passion and labour is to place value upon womanhood, so that we in turn can arise from a place of strength and cohesion and place value upon fellow humanity. For more information visit colourconference.com

We are a church that believes in reaching and influencing the world with the message of Jesus Christ. Hillsong Channel is an innovative media movement, beaming the timeless message of JESUS around the globe into television screens and digital devices to empower people in every sphere of life. This is a platform positioned in the heart of culture bringing JESUS into prisons and palaces all over the world. For more information visit hillsongchannel.com

Hillsong Television with Brian Houston is a half-hour Christian television program that features his teaching from Hillsong Church services. Pastor Brian's messages are empowering, passionate and practical for everyday life. His teaching will inspire you with the hope, joy, meaning and purpose that can be found in a personal and loving God. For more information visit hillsongtv.com

We are a church that believes in partnership and unity as we advance his kingdom on earth. The Hillsong Leadership Network is all about connecting, equipping and serving leaders, and exists to champion the cause of local churches everywhere. Our heart is that by coming alongside leaders, churches and ministries of varying denominations and styles, we are able to see more churches flourish and reach their God-given potential through this membership program. For more information visit hillsong.com/network

We are a church that believes in equipping people with principles and tools to lead and impact in every sphere of life. To find further information about the Pastoral Leadership Streams (including Youth, Children, Event Management, or Social Justice Pathways), Creative Streams (including Worship Music, TV & Media, Dance, or Production) or a Degree Program offered on campus by Alphacrucis College visit hillsongcollege.com

We are a church in many locations... Australia, Bali, Buenos Aires, Copenhagen, France, Germany, Israel, Kiev, Los Angeles, Moscow, Netherlands, New York City, Norway, Phoenix, Portugal, San Francisco, São Paulo, South Africa, Spain, Stockholm, Switzerland, UK.
For service times and information visit hillsong.com

TERMS AND CONDITIONS
Thank you for purchasing sheet music from Hillsong Music. Your purchase grants you the right to make ONE copy of the sheet music for your personal purposes (performances, worship services, personal study, musical teaching, etc). However the following rights have NOT been granted to you:
1. Reproduce copies of the sheet music in whole or in part outside of the rights granted to you above.
2. To translate, enhance, modify, alter or adapt the sheet music or any part of it for any purpose.
3. Cause or permit any third party to translate, enhance, modify, alter or adapt the sheet music or any part of it for any purpose.
4. Sub-licence, lease, lend, sell, rent, distribute or grant others any rights, or provide copies of the sheet music to others. Reproductions of the sheet music can be made for the purpose of church worship only with an existing Music Reproduction Licence from CCLI. For further information contact CCLI at http://www.ccli.com

For further information about copyright or other use of this music, please contact Hillsong Music Publishing at publishing@hillsong.com

TRANSCRIBED & ENGRAVED BY JARED HASCHEK

WHO YOU SAY I AM

Words and Music by
BEN FIELDING & REUBEN MORGAN

© 2017 Hillsong Music Publishing.
All rights reserved. International copyright secured. Used by permission.
Tel: +61 2 8853 5284 Email: publishing@hillsong.com CCLI Song No. 7102401

WHO YOU SAY I AM

Words and Music by
BEN FIELDING & REUBEN MORGAN

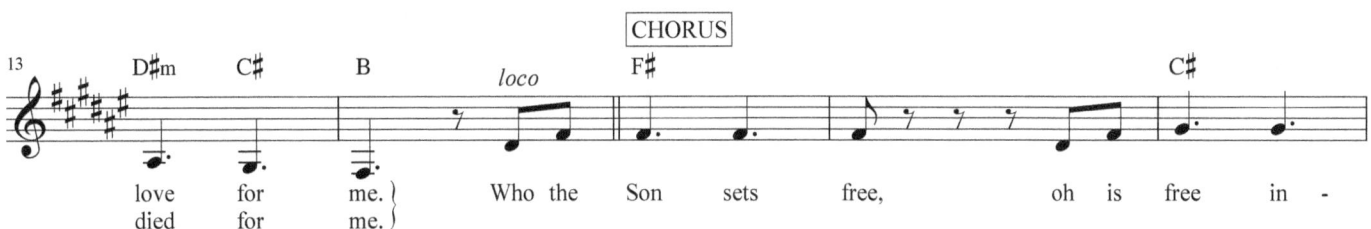

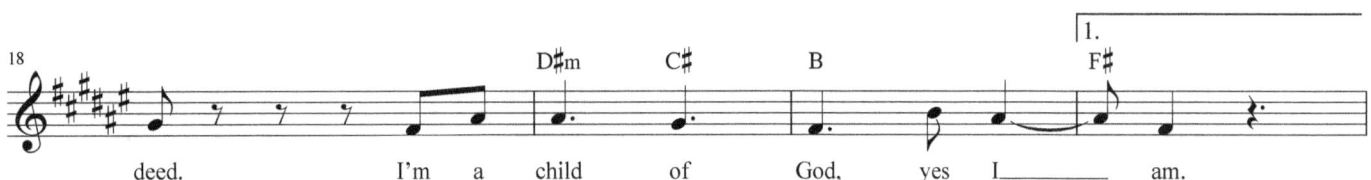

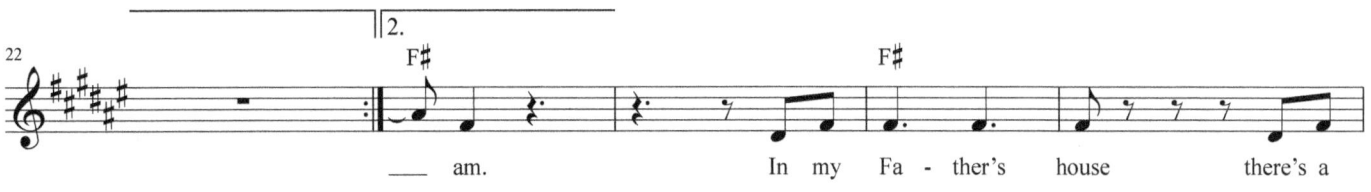

© 2017 Hillsong Music Publishing.
All rights reserved. International copyright secured. Used by permission.
Tel: +61 2 8853 5284 Email: publishing@hillsong.com CCLI Song No. 7102401

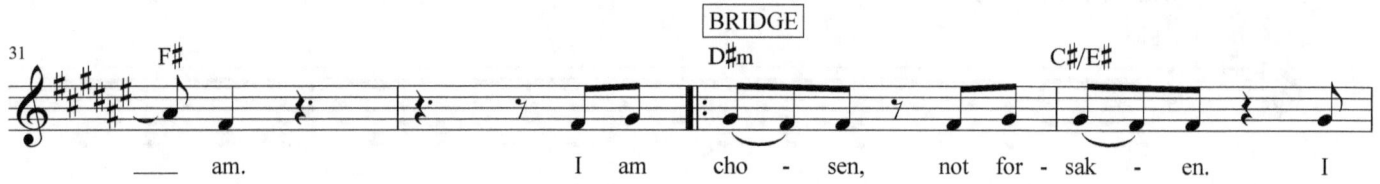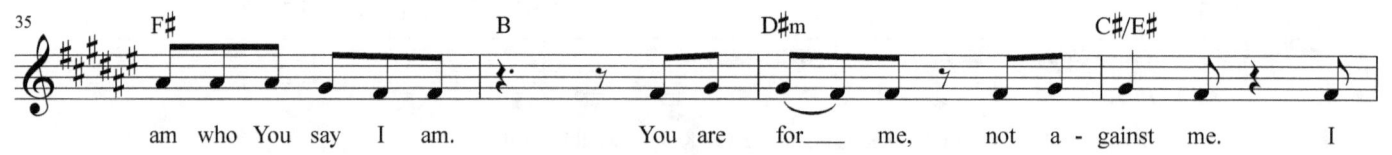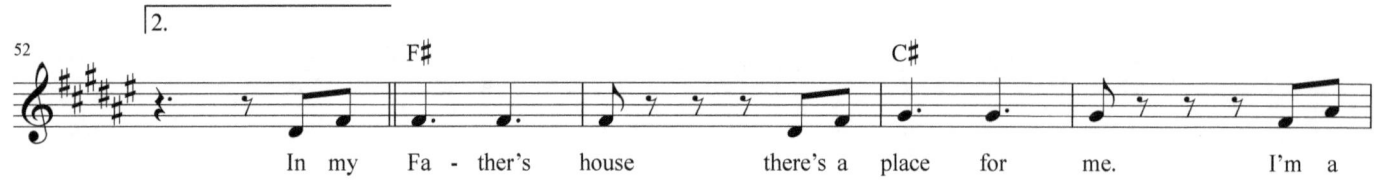

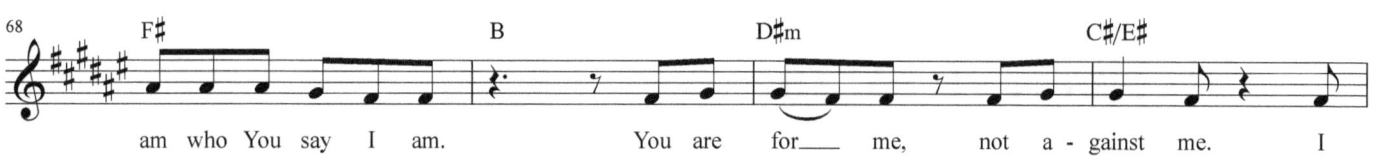

13

WHO YOU SAY I AM

**Words and Music by
Ben Fielding & Reuben Morgan**

VERSE 1:
Who am I that the highest King
Would welcome me
I was lost but He brought me in
Oh His love for me
Oh His love for me

CHORUS:
Who the Son sets free
Oh is free indeed
I'm a child of God
Yes I am

VERSE 2:
Free at last
He has ransomed me
His grace runs deep
While I was a slave to sin
Jesus died for me
Yes He died for me

© 2017 Hillsong Music Publishing
CCLI: 7102401

PO Box 1195 Castle Hill NSW 1765
Ph: +61 2 8853 5284 Fx: +61 2 8846 4625
E-mail: publishing@hillsong.com

CHORUS 2:
**Who the Son sets free
Oh is free indeed
I'm a child of God
Yes I am
In my Father's house
There's a place for me
I'm a child of God
Yes I am**

BRIDGE:
**I am chosen
Not forsaken
I am who You say I am
You are for me
Not against me
I am who You say I am**

YOU ARE LIFE

Words and Music by
BEN TAN, SCOTT LIGERTWOOD,
AODHAN KING & MICHAEL GUY CHISLETT

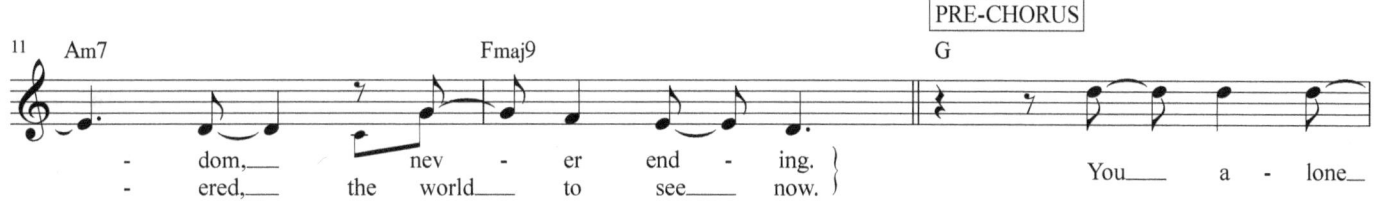

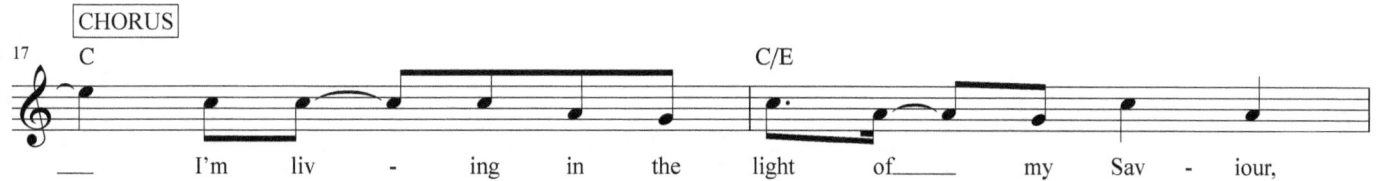

© 2017 Hillsong Music Publishing.
All rights reserved. International copyright secured. Used by permission.
Tel: +61 2 8853 5284 Email: publishing@hillsong.com CCLI Song No. 7102402

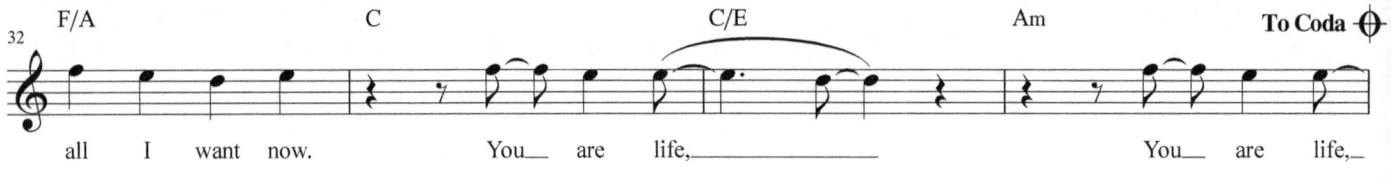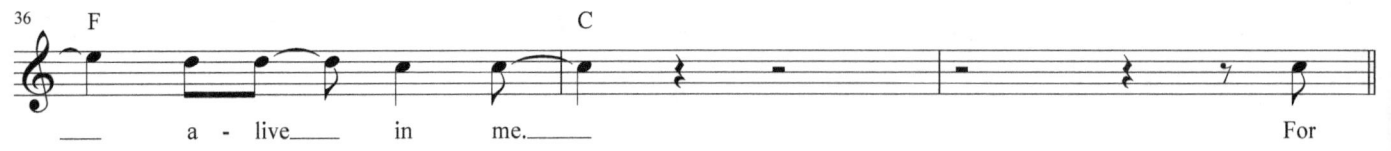

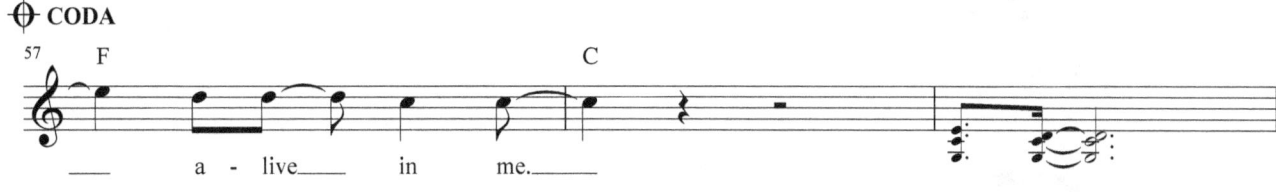

You Are Life

Words and Music by Ben Tan, Scott Ligertwood, Aodhan King & Michael Guy Chislett

VERSE 1:
You have come
And we have found life
Everlasting
Now alive
To know Your freedom
Never ending

PRE CHORUS:
You alone have made a way for us
In Your love
You are life

CHORUS:
I'm living in the light of my Saviour
Dancing in the arms of forever
I'm singing like I'm walking on water
You are life
Alive in me

© 2017 Hillsong Music Publishing
CCLI: 7102402

PO Box 1195 Castle Hill NSW 1765
Ph: +61 2 8853 5284 Fx: +61 2 8846 4625
E-mail: publishing@hillsong.com

VERSE 2:
From greyest skies
To living colour
You have called us
In Your life
Your light uncovered
The world to see now

POST - CHORUS:
I give my life to follow
'Cause Your love is all I want now
You are life
You are life
Alive in me

BRIDGE:
For all the world to find Your love
For all the world to see that You are God
Forever be lifted high

The One who holds the universe
And every beating heart across the earth
Jesus be lifted high

© 2017 Hillsong Music Publishing
CCLI: 7102402

PO Box 1195 Castle Hill NSW 1765
Ph: +61 2 8853 5284 Fx: +61 2 8846 4625
E-mail: publishing@hillsong.com

THE PASSION

Words and Music by
SCOTT LIGERTWOOD,
BROOKE LIGERTWOOD
& CHRIS DAVENPORT

VERSE 1/2

The pas - sion of our Sav - iour,
The In - no - cent judged guilt - y

the mer - cy of our God.
while the guilt - y one walks free.

The cross that leaves no ques - tion of the meas -
Death would be His por - tion and our por -

© 2017 Hillsong Music Publishing.
All rights reserved. International copyright secured. Used by permission.
Tel: +61 2 8853 5284 Email: publishing@hillsong.com CCLI Song No. 7102399

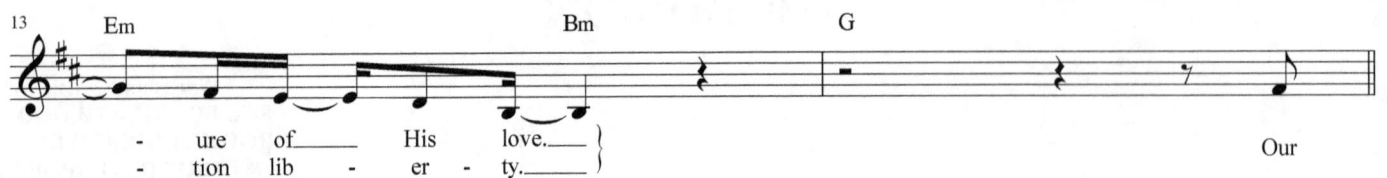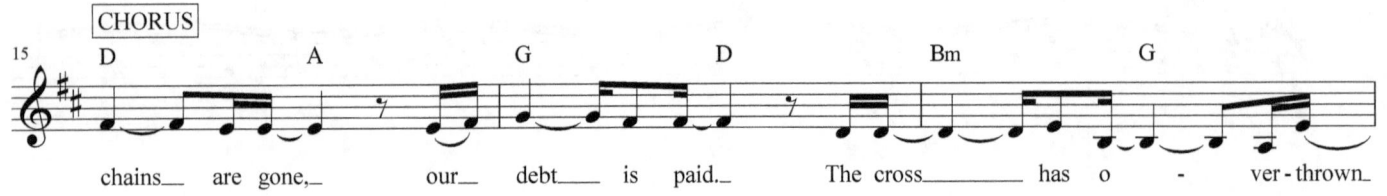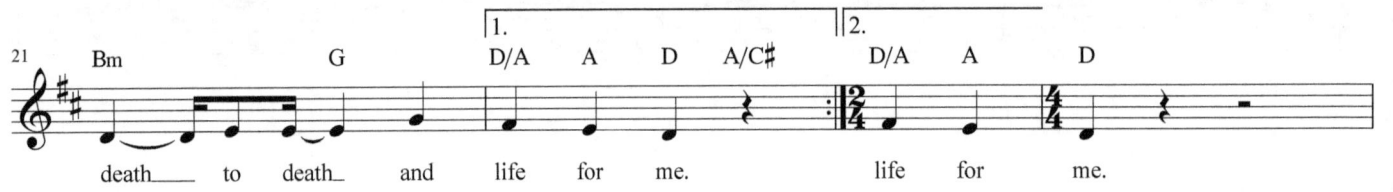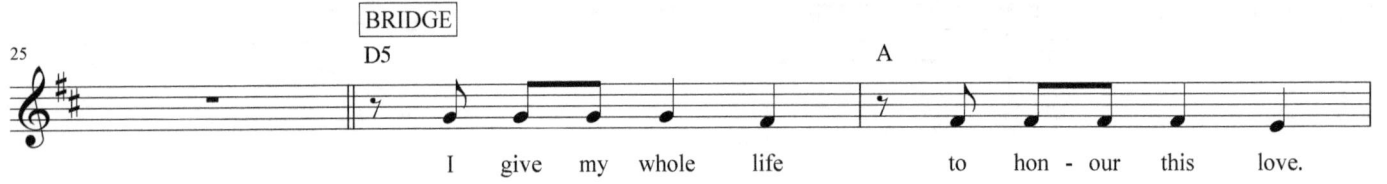

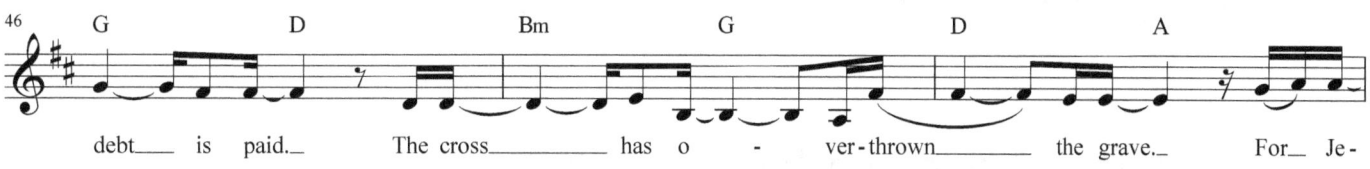

The Passion

**Words and Music by
Scott Ligertwood, Brooke Ligertwood
& Chris Davenport**

VERSE 1:
The passion of our Saviour
The mercy of our God
The cross that leaves no question
Of the measure of His love

CHORUS:
Our chains are gone
Our debt is paid
The cross has overthrown the grave
For Jesus' blood that sets us free
Means death to death
And life for me

VERSE 2:
The Innocent judged guilty
While the guilty one walks free
Death would be His portion
And our portion liberty

© 2017 Hillsong Music Publishing
CCLI: 7102399

PO Box 1195 Castle Hill NSW 1765
Ph: +61 2 8853 5284 Fx: +61 2 8846 4625
E-mail: publishing@hillsong.com

BRIDGE:
I give my whole life
To honour this love
By the Lamb who was slain
I'm forgiven

The sinner's Saviour
Crown Him forever
For the Lamb who was slain
He is risen

© 2017 Hillsong Music Publishing
CCLI: 7102399

PO Box 1195 Castle Hill NSW 1765
Ph: +61 2 8853 5284 Fx: +61 2 8846 4625
E-mail: publishing@hillsong.com

GOD SO LOVED

Words and Music by
MATT CROCKER &
MARTY SAMPSON

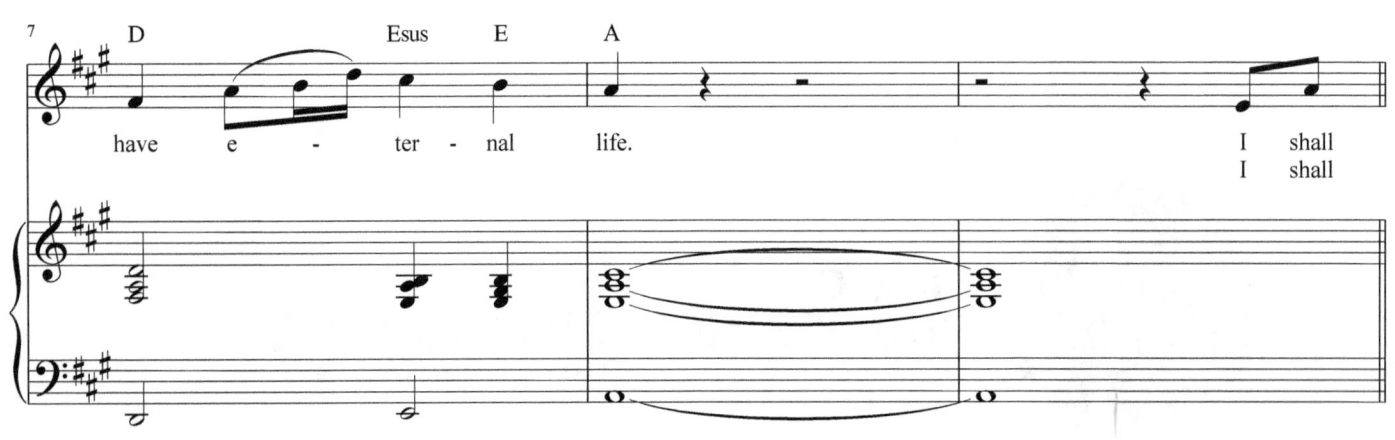

© 2017 Hillsong Music Publishing.
All rights reserved. International copyright secured. Used by permission.
Tel: +61 2 8853 5284 Email: publishing@hillsong.com CCLI Song No. 7102394

GOD SO LOVED

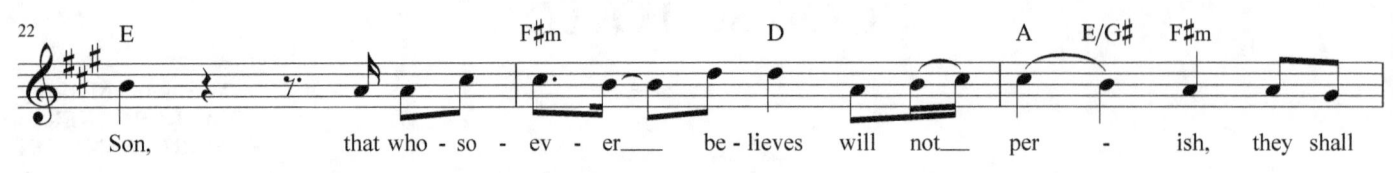

GOD SO LOVED

**Words and Music by
Matt Crocker & Marty Sampson**

VERSE 1:
I shall hold
To the cross
I shall hold
To God alone

For His love
Has salvaged me
For His love
Has set me free

CHORUS:
For God so loved the world
That He gave His only Son
Whosoever believes
Will not perish
They shall have eternal life

© 2017 Hillsong Music Publishing
CCLI: 7102394

PO Box 1195 Castle Hill NSW 1765
Ph: +61 2 8853 5284 Fx: +61 2 8846 4625
E-mail: publishing@hillsong.com

VERSE 2:
I shall wait
Upon the Lord
I shall wait
Upon His Word

By His grace
I am released
By His grace
I am redeemed

BRIDGE:
By His precious blood
I have been set free
For the glory of Jesus' Name

I surrender all
Now to Christ alone
In Jesus I am saved

© 2017 Hillsong Music Publishing
CCLI: 7102394

PO Box 1195 Castle Hill NSW 1765
Ph: +61 2 8853 5284 Fx: +61 2 8846 4625
E-mail: publishing@hillsong.com

BE STILL

Words and Music by Ben Fielding & Reuben Morgan

VERSE 1:
Be still and know
That the Lord is in control
Be still my soul
Stand and watch as giants fall

CHORUS:
I won't be afraid
You are here
You silence all my fear
I won't be afraid
You don't let go
Be still my heart and know
I won't be afraid

VERSE 2:
Be still and trust
What the Lord has said is done
Find rest don't strive
Watch as faith and grace align

© 2017 Hillsong Music Publishing
CCLI: 7102393

PO Box 1195 Castle Hill NSW 1765
Ph: +61 2 8853 5284 Fx: +61 2 8846 4625
E-mail: publishing@hillsong.com

BRIDGE:
Surely love and mercy
Your peace and kindness
Will follow me
Will follow me

POST CHORUS:
Your love surrounds me
Your love surrounds me here

© 2017 Hillsong Music Publishing
CCLI: 7102393

PO Box 1195 Castle Hill NSW 1765
Ph: +61 2 8853 5284 Fx: +61 2 8846 4625
E-mail: publishing@hillsong.com

REMEMBRANCE

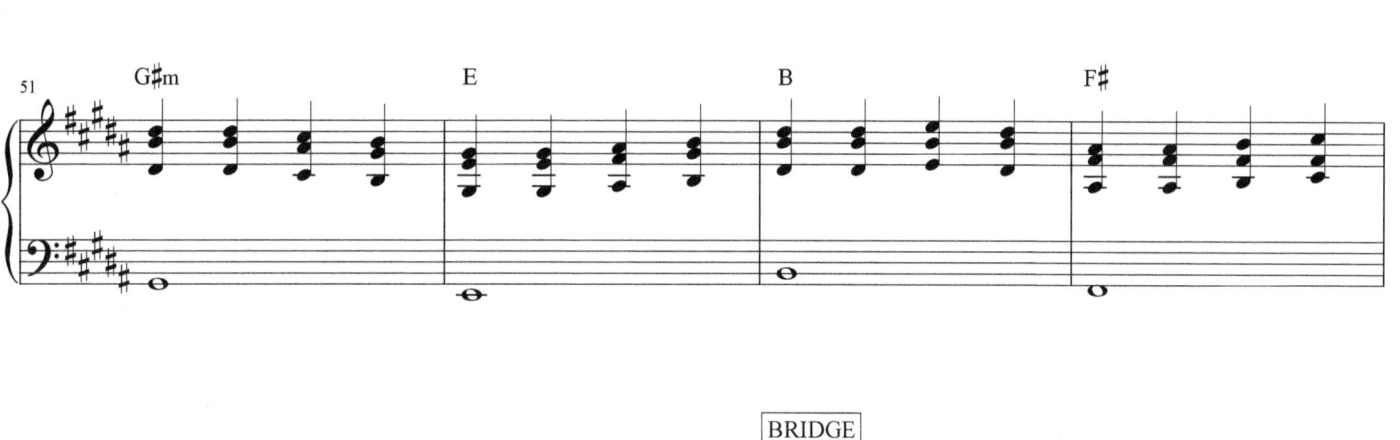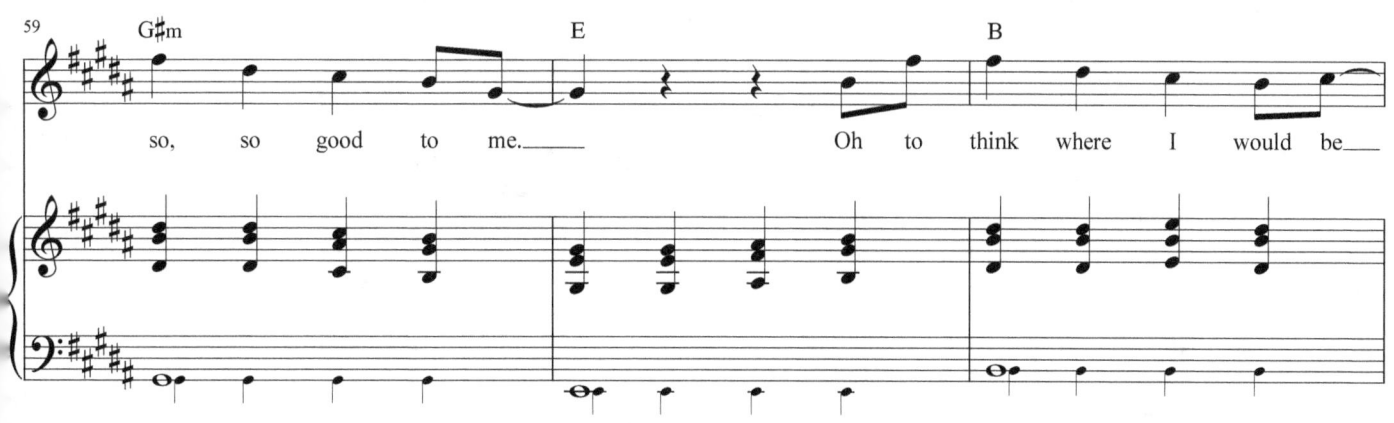

Remembrance

**Words and Music by
Chris Davenport & Benjamin Hastings**

VERSE 1:
I take the bread of life
Broken for all my sin
Your body crucified
To make me whole again

VERSE 2:
I will recall the cup
Poured out in sacrifice
To trade this sinners' end
For Your new covenant

CHORUS:
Hallelujah
I'll live my life in remembrance
Hallelujah
Your promise I won't forget

© 2017 Hillsong Music Publishing
CCLI: 7102398

PO Box 1195 Castle Hill NSW 1765
Ph: +61 2 8853 5284 Fx: +61 2 8846 4625
E-mail: publishing@hillsong.com

VERSE 3:
I'll walk salvation's road
With fear and trembling
Your way borne as my own
As Christ is formed in me

POST-CHORUS 1:
If ever I should lose my way
If ever I deny Your grace
Remind me of the price You paid
Hallelujah
I'll live in remembrance

BRIDGE (repeated):
You've been so so good to me
You've been so so good to me
Oh to think where I would be
If not for You
If not for You

© 2017 Hillsong Music Publishing
CCLI: 7102398

PO Box 1195 Castle Hill NSW 1765
Ph: +61 2 8853 5284 Fx: +61 2 8846 4625
E-mail: publishing@hillsong.com

POST-CHORUS 2:
As far as heights reach from the depths
As far as east is from the west
So far Your grace has carried me

POST-CHORUS 3:
Until I see You face to face
Until at last I've won my race
Remind me You're not finished yet

TAG:
Hallelujah
Hallelujah
Hallelujah
I'll live in remembrance

© 2017 Hillsong Music Publishing
CCLI: 7102398

PO Box 1195 Castle Hill NSW 1765
Ph: +61 2 8853 5284 Fx: +61 2 8846 4625
E-mail: publishing@hillsong.com

VALENTINE

**Words and Music by
BROOKE LIGERTWOOD,
SCOTT LIGERTWOOD
& JOEL HOUSTON**

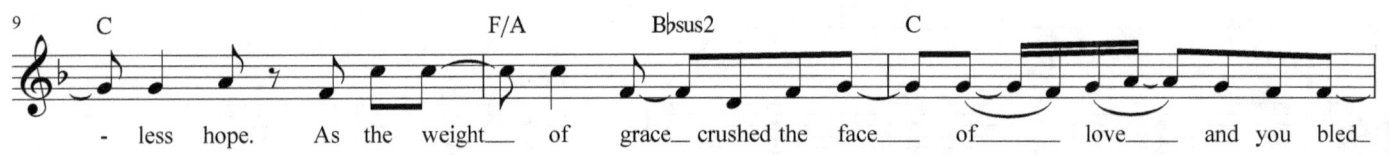
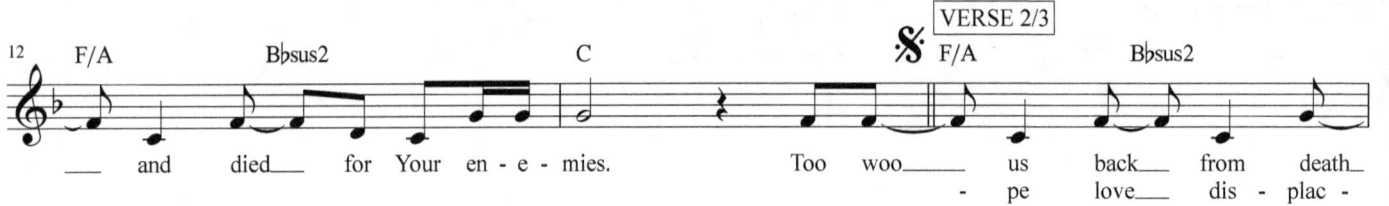
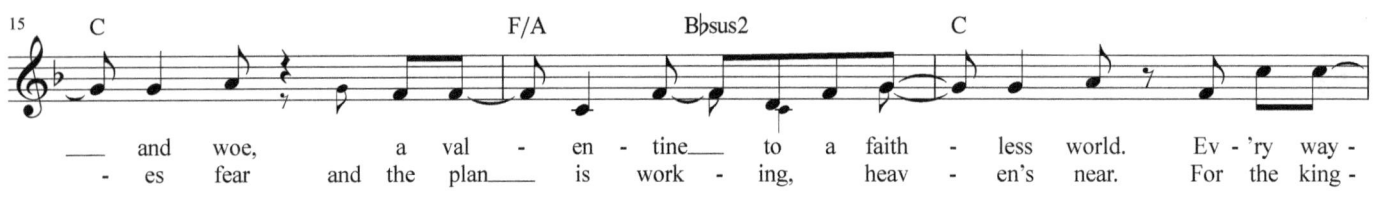

© 2017 Hillsong Music Publishing.
All rights reserved. International copyright secured. Used by permission.
Tel: +61 2 8853 5284 Email: publishing@hillsong.com CCLI Song No. 7102400

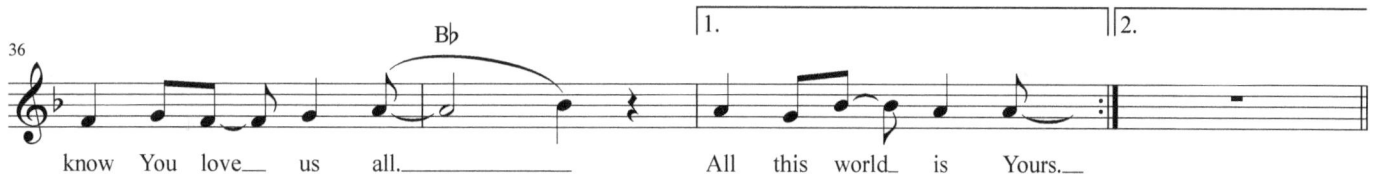

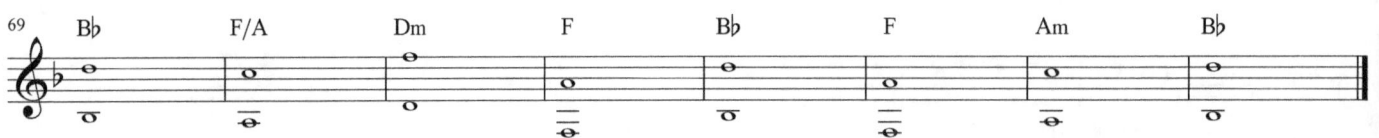

VALENTINE

**Words and Music by
Brooke Ligertwood, Scott Ligertwood
& Joel Houston**

VERSE 1:
From Your sacrifice for the sake of all
Redemption's birth and relentless hope
As the weight of grace crushed the face of love
And You bled and died for Your enemies

VERSE 2:
To woo us back from death and woe
A valentine to a faithless world
Every wayward heart You pursue us all
And in kindness call us home

CHORUS:
This world is Yours
My God this world is Yours
All You made to be Yours
I know You love us all

© 2017 Hillsong Music Publishing
CCLI: 7102400

PO Box 1195 Castle Hill NSW 1765
Ph: +61 2 8853 5284 Fx: +61 2 8846 4625
E-mail: publishing@hillsong.com

VERSE 3:
Your agape love displaces fear
And the plan is working heaven's near
For the kingdom comes to the heart that whispers
Have mercy God on me

CHORUS 2:
This world is Yours
My God this world is Yours
All You made to be Yours
I know You love us all

All this world is Yours
My God this world is Yours
All You made to be Yours
I know You love us all

BRIDGE:
You reign forever
You reign forevermore
My heart surrendered
You reign forevermore

© 2017 Hillsong Music Publishing
CCLI: 7102400

PO Box 1195 Castle Hill NSW 1765
Ph: +61 2 8853 5284 Fx: +61 2 8846 4625
E-mail: publishing@hillsong.com

TOUCH OF HEAVEN

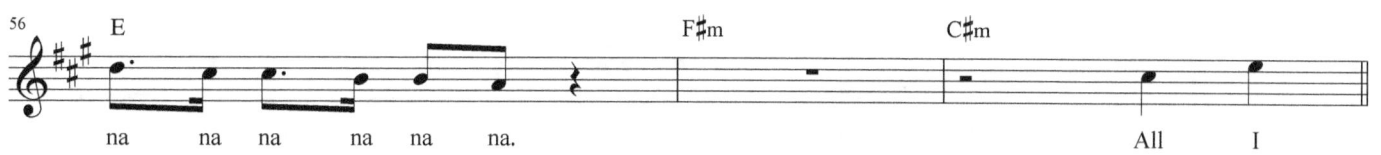
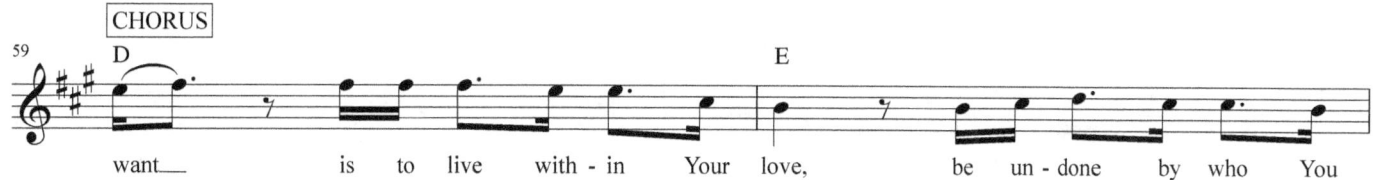

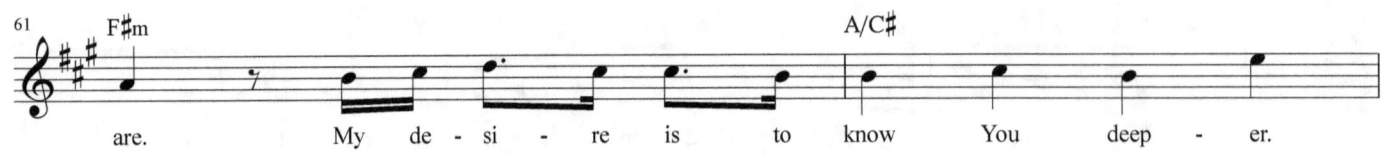

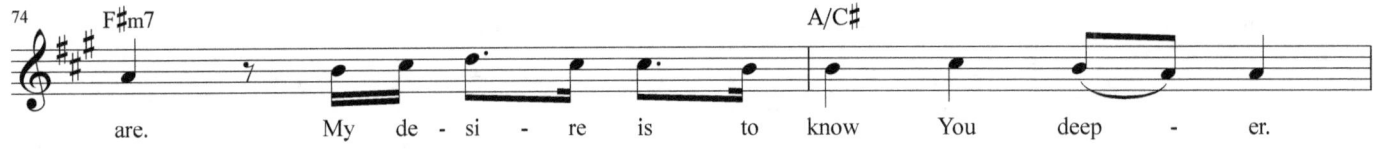
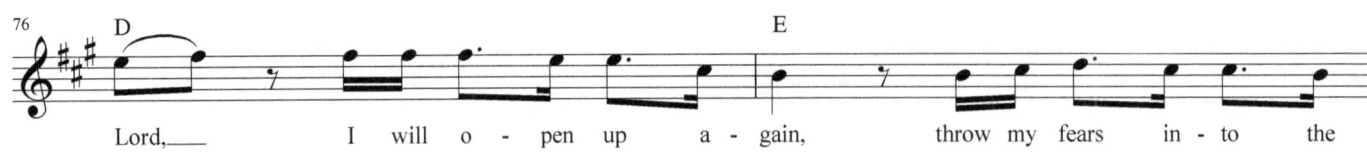

TOUCH OF HEAVEN

**Words and Music by
Hannah Hobbs, Aodhan King
& Michael Fatkin**

VERSE 1:
How I live for the moments
Where I'm still in Your presence
All the noise dies down
Lord speak to me now

You have all my attention
I will linger and listen
I can't miss a thing

PRE-CHORUS:
Lord I know my heart wants more of You
My heart wants something new
So I surrender all

© 2017 Hillsong Music Publishing
CCLI: 7102403

PO Box 1195 Castle Hill NSW 1765
Ph: +61 2 8853 5284 Fx: +61 2 8846 4625
E-mail: publishing@hillsong.com

CHORUS:
All I want is to live within Your love
Be undone by who You are
My desire is to know You deeper
Lord I will open up again
Throw my fears into the wind
I am desperate for a touch of heaven

VERSE 2:
You're the fire in the morning
You're the cool in the evening
The breath in my soul
The life in my bones

There is no hesitation
In Your love and affection
It's the sweetest of all

BRIDGE:
I open up my heart to You
I open up my heart to You now
So do what only You can
Jesus have Your way in me now

© 2017 Hillsong Music Publishing
CCLI: 7102403

PO Box 1195 Castle Hill NSW 1765
Ph: +61 2 8853 5284 Fx: +61 2 8846 4625
E-mail: publishing@hillsong.com

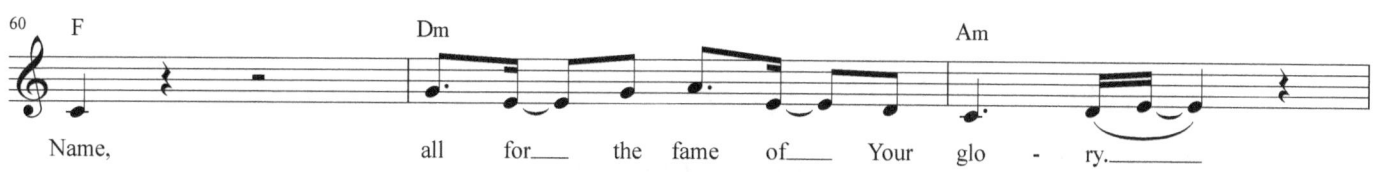

LETTERED LOVE

**Words and Music by
Nathan Hughes & Scott Ligertwood**

VERSE 1:
Your Word shows
How much You have loved me
Sending Love to find me
Reaching to my heart

Now I see
Lettered love has found me
Littered red with mercy
Written in Your scars
Jesus

CHORUS 1:
So have this broken heart
And show me what Love paid for
Oh Lord let my heart beat with Yours
This lettered love
Is shaping my story

© 2017 Hillsong Music Publishing
CCLI: 7102395

PO Box 1195 Castle Hill NSW 1765
Ph: +61 2 8853 5284 Fx: +61 2 8846 4625
E-mail: publishing@hillsong.com

TAG:

All for the praise of Your Name
All for the fame of Your glory
Jesus be all that I seek
Your presence is all that I need

BRIDGE:

Like the sun and moon
Like the night and noon
Your Word is light to me
And I'll praise You

Splitting death and life
Like the earth and sky
Your Word is light in me
And I'll praise You

CHORUS 2:

Lord have this broken heart
For this broken heart is paid for
And shaped by the truth of Your Word
This lettered love
Has written my story

© 2017 Hillsong Music Publishing
CCLI: 7102395

PO Box 1195 Castle Hill NSW 1765
Ph: +61 2 8853 5284 Fx: +61 2 8846 4625
E-mail: publishing@hillsong.com

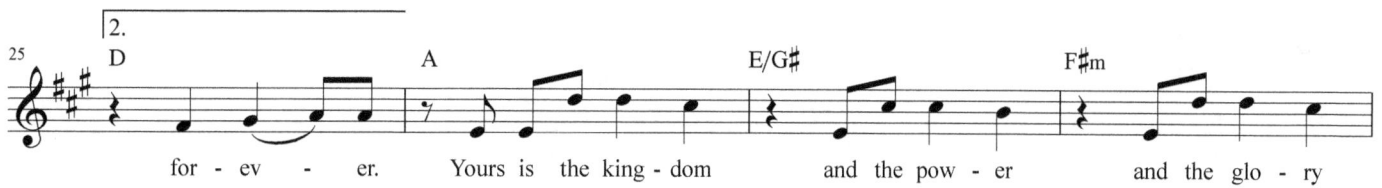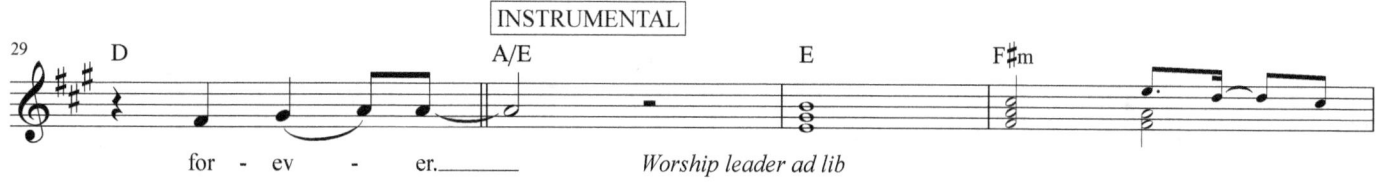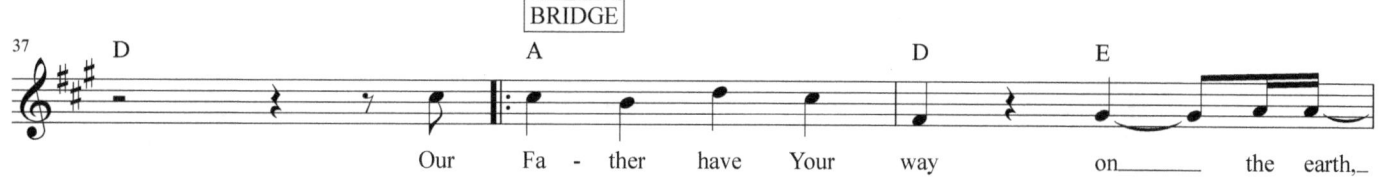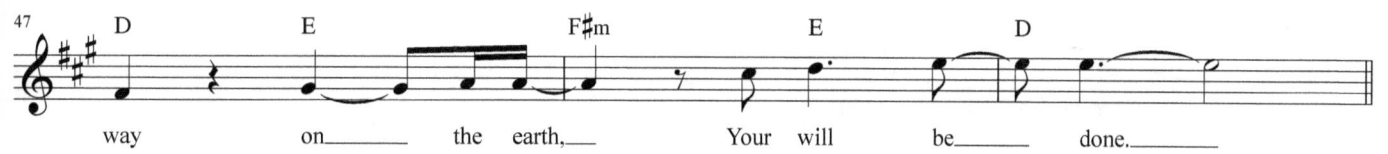

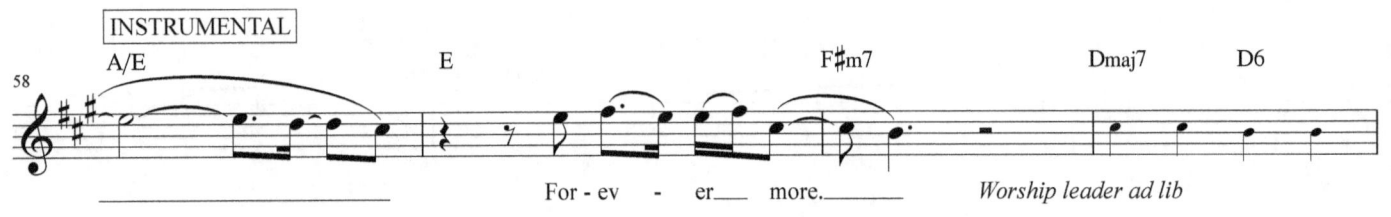

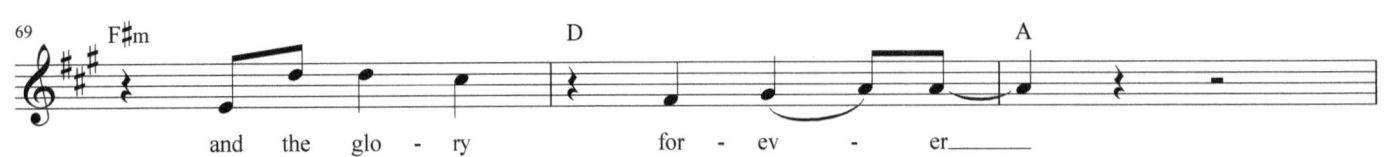

The Lord's Prayer

**Words and Music by
Ben Fielding, Benjamin Hastings,
Reuben Morgan & Marty Sampson**

VERSE 1:
Father in Heaven
Holy is Your Name
Your kingdom come
Your will be done on earth
As it is in Heaven
Our Father in Heaven

PRE-CHORUS:
Lead us not into temptation
God deliver us from the enemy

CHORUS:
Yours is the kingdom
And the power and the glory
Forever

© 2017 Hillsong Music Publishing
CCLI: 7102396

PO Box 1195 Castle Hill NSW 1765
Ph: +61 2 8853 5284 Fx: +61 2 8846 4625
E-mail: publishing@hillsong.com

VERSE 2:
Give us each moment
All that we need
Forgive us our sins
As we forgive the ones
Who have sinned against us
Our Father in Heaven

BRIDGE:
Our Father have Your way
On the earth
Your will be done

Tag:
And evermore
Amen

© 2017 Hillsong Music Publishing
CCLI: 7102396

PO Box 1195 Castle Hill NSW 1765
Ph: +61 2 8853 5284 Fx: +61 2 8846 4625
E-mail: publishing@hillsong.com

NEW WINE

Words and Music by
BROOKE LIGERTWOOD

© 2017 Hillsong Music Publishing.
All rights reserved. International copyright secured. Used by permission.
Tel: +61 2 8853 5284 Email: publishing@hillsong.com CCLI Song No. 7102397

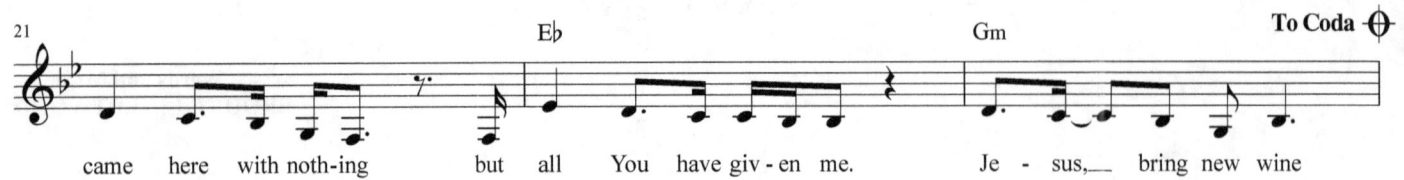
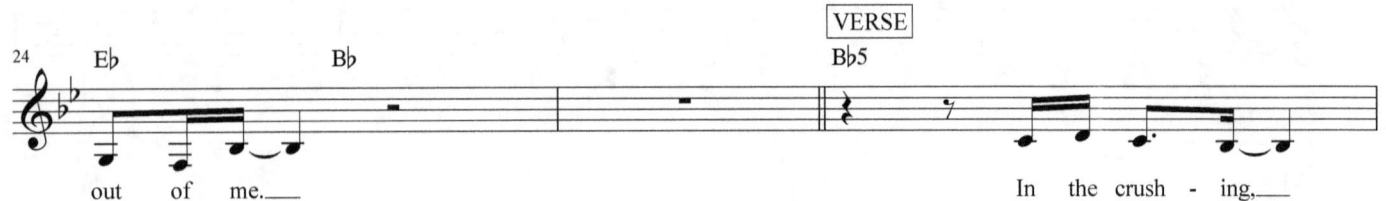

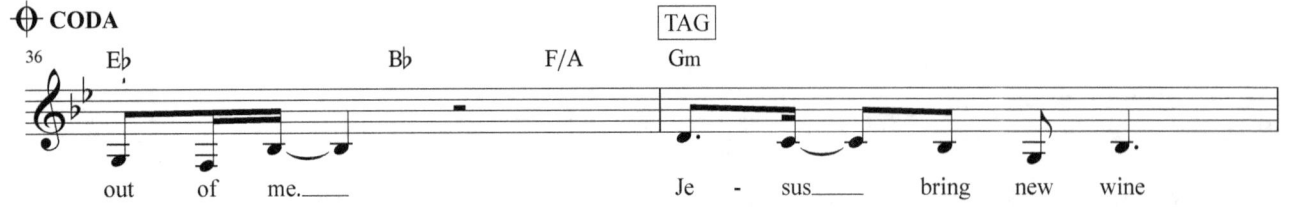

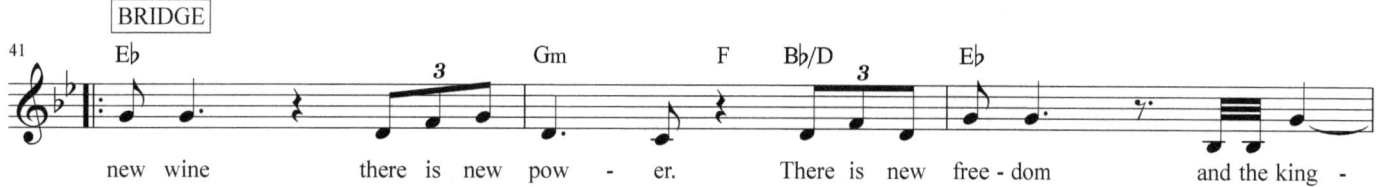

NEW WINE

**Words and Music by
Brooke Ligertwood**

VERSE 1:
**In the crushing
In the pressing
You are making new wine
In the soil I now surrender
You are breaking new ground**

PRE-CHORUS:
**So I yield to You and to Your careful hand
When I trust You I don't need to understand**

CHORUS:
**Make me Your vessel
Make me an offering
Make me whatever You want me to be
I came here with nothing
But all You have given me
Jesus bring new wine out of me**

© 2017 Hillsong Music Publishing
CCLI: 7102397

PO Box 1195 Castle Hill NSW 1765
Ph: +61 2 8853 5284 Fx: +61 2 8846 4625
E-mail: publishing@hillsong.com

VERSE 2:
In the crushing
In the pressing
You are making new wine
In the soil I now surrender
You are breaking new ground

VERSE TAG:
You are breaking new ground

BRIDGE:
Where there is new wine
There is new power
There is new freedom
The Kingdom is here
I lay down my old flames
To carry Your new fire today

© 2017 Hillsong Music Publishing
CCLI: 7102397

PO Box 1195 Castle Hill NSW 1765
Ph: +61 2 8853 5284 Fx: +61 2 8846 4625
E-mail: publishing@hillsong.com

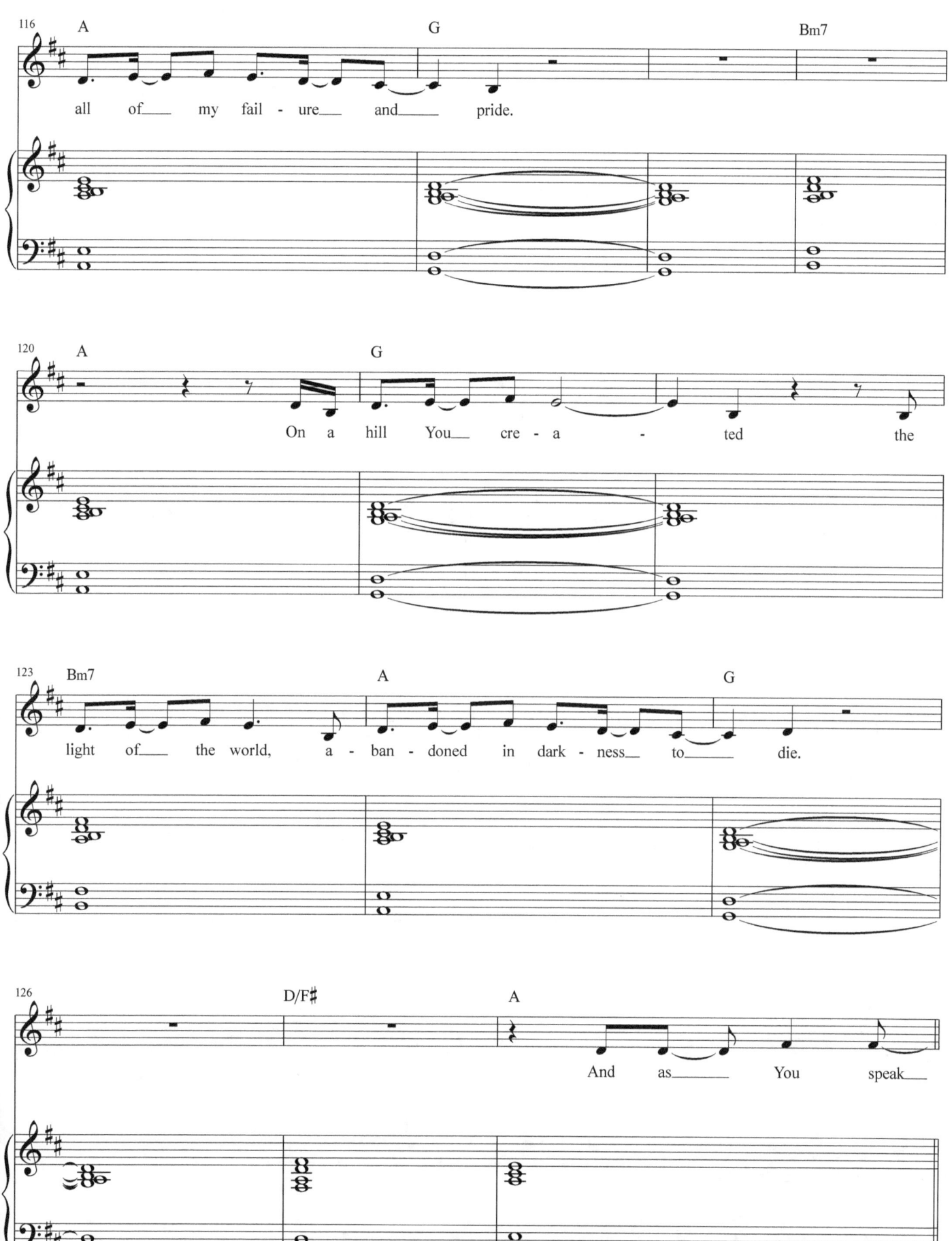

SO WILL I (100 BILLION X)

Words and Music by
JOEL HOUSTON, BENJAMIN HASTINGS
& MICHAEL FATKIN

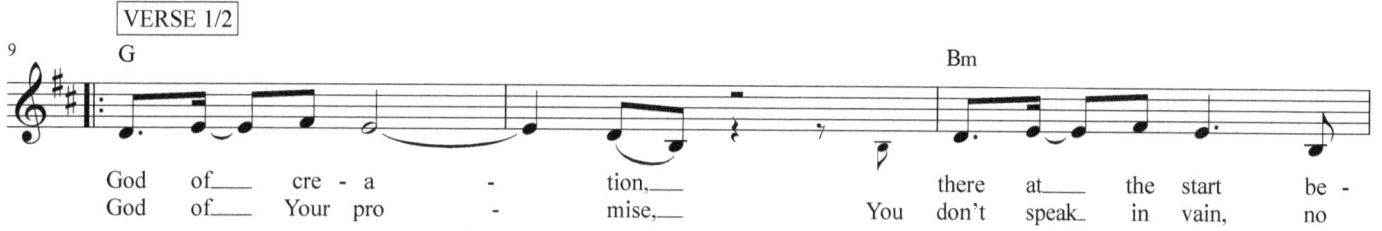

God of cre - a - tion, there at the start be -
God of Your pro - mise, You don't speak in vain, no

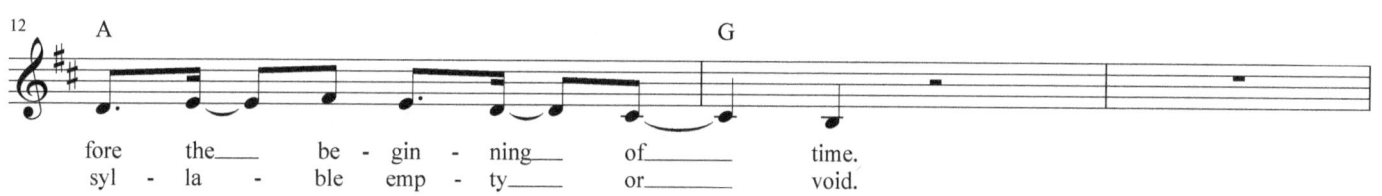

fore the be - gin - ning of time.
syl - la - ble emp - ty or void.

With no point of ref -
For once You have spo -

- 'rence, You spoke to the dark and fleshed out the won - der of
- ken, all na - ture and sci - ence fol - low the sound of Your

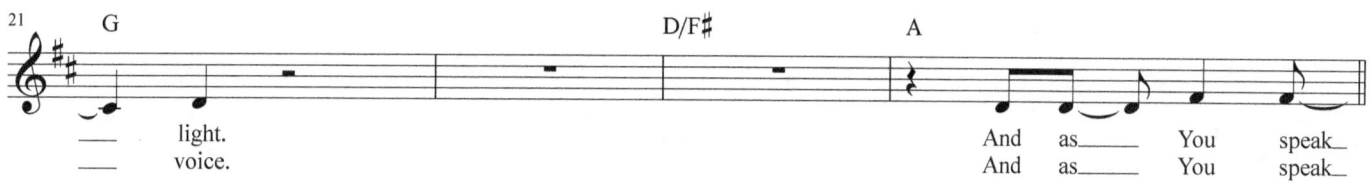

light. And as You speak
voice. And as You speak

© 2017 Hillsong Music Publishing.
All rights reserved. International copyright secured. Used by permission.
Tel: +61 2 8853 5284 Email: publishing@hillsong.com CCLI Song No. 7084123

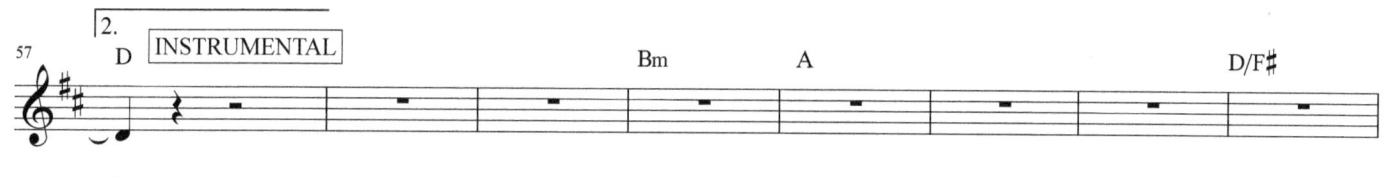

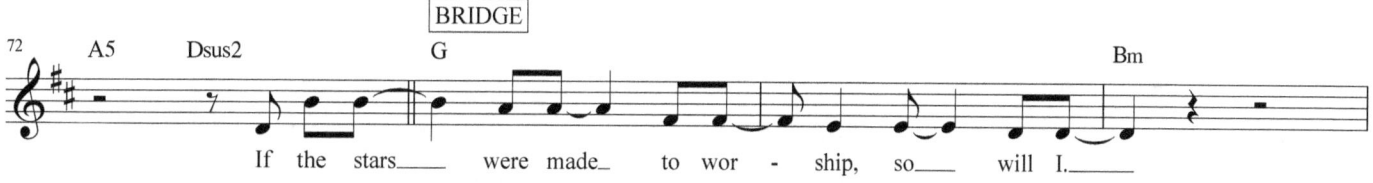

If the stars were made to worship, so will I.

If the mountains bow in rev-'rence, so will I.

If the oceans roar Your great-ness, so will I.

For if ev-'ry-thing exists to lift You high, so will I.

If the wind goes where You send it, so will I.

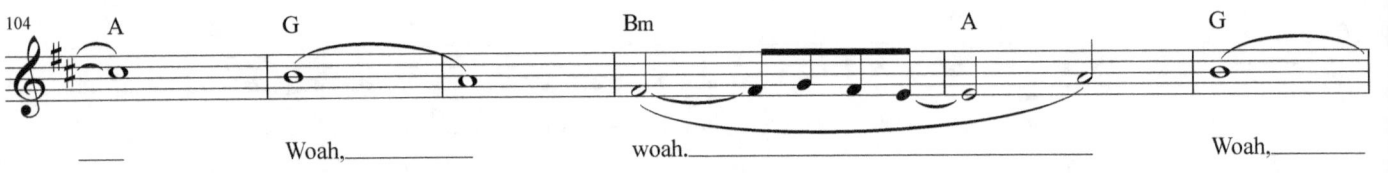

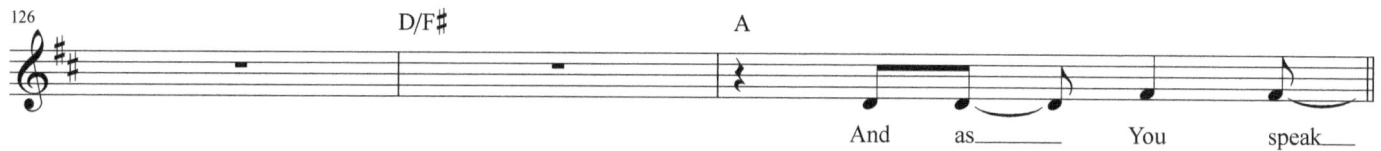

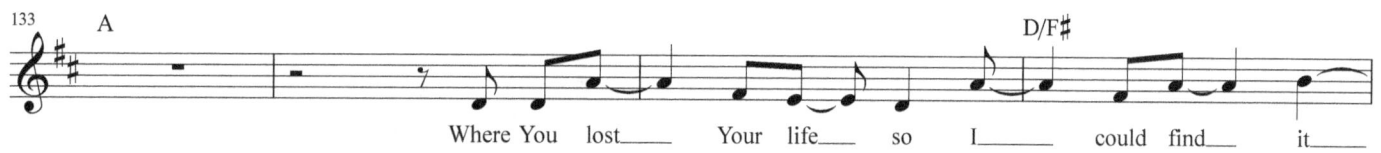
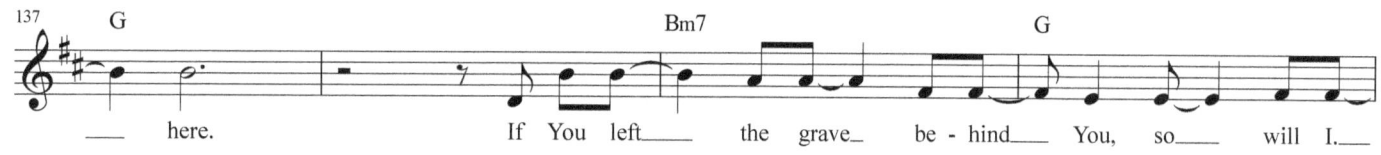

SO WILL I (100 BILLION X)

**Words and Music by Joel Houston
Benjamin Hastings & Michael Fatkin**

VERSE 1:
God of creation
There at the start
Before the beginning of time
With no point of reference
You spoke to the dark
And fleshed out the wonder of light

CHORUS 1:
And as You speak
A hundred billion galaxies are born
In the vapour of Your breath the planets form
If the stars were made to worship so will I
I can see Your heart in everything You've made
Every burning star
A signal fire of grace
If creation sings Your praises so will I

© 2017 Hillsong Music Publishing
CCLI: 7084123

PO Box 1195 Castle Hill NSW 1765
Ph: +61 2 8853 5284 Fx: +61 2 8846 4625
E-mail: publishing@hillsong.com

VERSE 2:
God of Your promise
You don't speak in vain
No syllable empty or void
For once You have spoken
All nature and science
Follow the sound of Your voice

CHORUS 2:
And as You speak
A hundred billion creatures catch Your breath
Evolving in pursuit of what You said
If it all reveals Your nature so will I
I can see Your heart in everything You say
Every painted sky
A canvas of Your grace
If creation still obeys You so will I

© 2017 Hillsong Music Publishing
CCLI: 7084123

PO Box 1195 Castle Hill NSW 1765
Ph: +61 2 8853 5284 Fx: +61 2 8846 4625
E-mail: publishing@hillsong.com

BRIDGE:
If the stars were made to worship so will I
If the mountains bow in reverence so will I
If the oceans roar Your greatness so will I
For if everything exists to lift You high so will I

If the wind goes where You send it so will I
If the rocks cry out in silence so will I
If the sum of all our praises still falls shy
Then we'll sing again a hundred billion times

VERSE 3:
God of salvation
You chased down my heart
Through all of my failure and pride
On a hill You created
The light of the world
Abandoned in darkness to die

© 2017 Hillsong Music Publishing
CCLI: 7084123

PO Box 1195 Castle Hill NSW 1765
Ph: +61 2 8853 5284 Fx: +61 2 8846 4625
E-mail: publishing@hillsong.com

So Will I (100 Billion X) – Page 4

CHORUS 3:
And as You speak
A hundred billion failures disappear
Where You lost Your life so I could find it here
If You left the grave behind You so will I
I can see Your heart in everything You've done
Every part designed in a work of art called love
If You gladly chose surrender so will I

I can see Your heart
Eight billion different ways
Every precious one
A child You died to save
If You gave Your life to love them so will I

TAG:
Like You would again a hundred billion times
But what measure could amount to Your desire
You're the One who never leaves the one behind

© 2017 Hillsong Music Publishing
CCLI: 7084123

PO Box 1195 Castle Hill NSW 1765
Ph: +61 2 8853 5284 Fx: +61 2 8846 4625
E-mail: publishing@hillsong.com

www.ingramcontent.com/pod-product-compliance
Lightning Source LLC
Chambersburg PA
CBHW080807300426
44114CB00020B/2863